Michael Phelps

ABDO
Publishing Company

A Big Buddy Book
by **Sarah Tieck**

VISIT US AT
www.abdopublishing.com

Published by ABDO Publishing Company, 8000 West 78th Street, Edina, Minnesota 55439.

Printed in the United States.

Coordinating Series Editor: Rochelle Baltzer
Contributing Editor: Marcia Zappa
Graphic Design: Maria Hosley
Cover Photograph: *AP Photo*: Mark J. Terrill
Interior Photographs/Illustrations: *AP Photo*: AP Photo (pp. 23, 25), Mark Baker (pp. 23, 29), Rick Bowmer (p. 17),
    EFE/Andrue Dalmau (p. 19), Richard Drew (p. 27), Itsuo Inouye (p. 15), Rusty Kennedy (p. 20), Thomas Kienzle
    (p. 17), David J. Phillip (p. 13), Amy Sancetta (p. 17), Sipa via AP Images (pp. 4, 17), Mark J. Terrill (pp. 11, 20),
    USOC (p. 9); *Getty Images*: Martin Bureau/AFP (p. 7), Ezra Shaw (p. 12).

Library of Congress Cataloging-in-Publication Data

Tieck, Sarah, 1976-
  Michael Phelps / Sarah Tieck.
     p. cm. -- (Big buddy biographies)
  ISBN 978-1-60453-550-1
  1. Phelps, Michael, 1985---Juvenile literature. 2. Swimmers--United States--Biography--Juvenile literature. 3.
Olympics--Juvenile literature. I. Title.
  GV838.P54T45 2009
  797.2'1092--dc22
  [B]
                                            2008038046

Michael
Phelps

Contents

In 2008, Michael won eight gold medals at the Olympics. No one has ever won this many in one year!

Swimming Sensation

Michael Phelps is a famous swimmer. He has won races at the Olympics, the World **Championships**, and the Pan Pacific Championships. Some say he is the best swimmer ever.

Pennsylvania

New Jersey

Maryland
Baltimore

West Virginia

Virginia

Delaware

ATLANTIC OCEAN

Family Ties

Michael Fred Phelps was born in Baltimore, Maryland, on June 30, 1985. His parents are Fred and Debbie Phelps. His older sisters are Hilary and Whitney.

When Michael was nine, his parents divorced. Life changed for Michael, Hilary, and Whitney.

Today Whitney, Debbie, and Hilary (*left to right*) often attend Michael's races.

School was hard for Michael. Other kids
often teased and picked on him. During
elementary school, his family discovered he had
attention-deficit/hyperactivity disorder (ADHD).
People with ADHD struggle to pay attention. This
made learning harder for Michael.

Michael attended Towson High School until graduating in 2003.

9

Early Years

The Phelps children were good swimmers. Michael often watched his sisters practice and race. In 1996, Whitney almost went to the Olympics! Later, she hurt her back and had to quit swimming.

When Michael was seven, he also started swimming. At first, he was afraid to put his face in the water. So, his **coaches** taught him to float on his back. Soon, he could do the backstroke. And, his swimming skills grew.

Bob is still Michael's coach. Sometimes, they train for five hours a day!

When Michael was about 11, he began working with coach Bob Bowman. They trained every day at the North Baltimore Aquatic Club.

Sometimes Michael didn't want to train. But, Bob pushed him. He noticed Michael's unusual body and swimming skill. He believed Michael would become a great swimmer.

Michael learned the four types of swimming strokes for racing. These are the backstroke, breaststroke, butterfly, and freestyle.

Big Dreams

In 1996, Michael attended the Summer Olympics in Atlanta, Georgia. There, he saw famous swimmers from around the world. He wanted to swim in the Olympics, too!

By 1999, Michael had made the U.S. National B Team. Soon after, he made the Olympic Swim Team! In 2000, he raced in the Summer Olympics in Sydney, Australia.

Tom Machlow was one of the swimmers Michael saw at the 1996 Olympics. Later, Tom and Michael became teammates.

The Olympic Games

The Olympic Games are a famous worldwide sports **competition**. The Olympics happen every two years, changing between the Summer Olympics and the Winter Olympics. People from around the world compete to win Olympic events. First-place winners receive gold **medals**. Silver medals are given to second-place winners. And, third-place winners receive bronze medals.

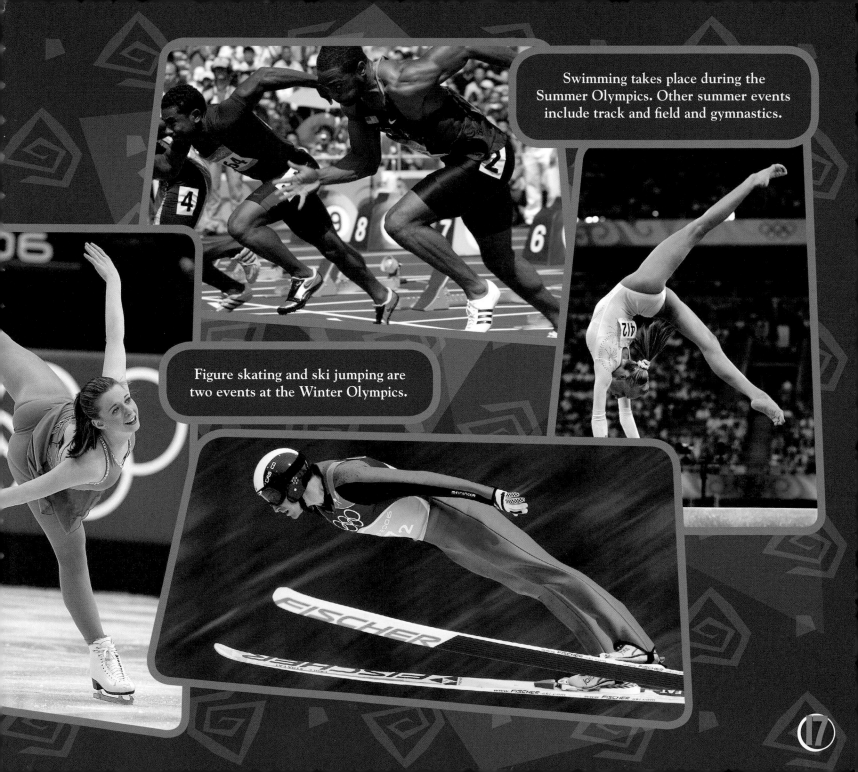

Swimming takes place during the Summer Olympics. Other summer events include track and field and gymnastics.

Figure skating and ski jumping are two events at the Winter Olympics.

Olympic Champion

In 2001, Michael became a **professional** swimmer. People began to notice him. Michael raced in national and worldwide events. He won **medals** and broke records. He also began training for the 2004 Olympics.

Michael won four gold and two silver medals at the World Swimming Championships in 2003.

19

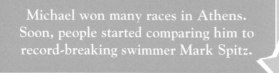
Michael won many races in Athens. Soon, people started comparing him to record-breaking swimmer Mark Spitz.

In addition to winning medals, Michael set a world record for speed in the 400-meter individual medley!

Did you know...

The first Olympic Games were held in 776 BC in Olympia, Greece. Centuries later, people decided to start the Olympics again. In 1896, the first modern games took place in Athens.

In 2004, Michael raced in the Summer Olympics in Athens, Greece. He was outstanding! He won six gold and two bronze medals.

After the Olympics, Michael moved to Ann Arbor, Michigan. There, he attended the University of Michigan. He also continued training with Bob.

Record Breaker

In 2008, Michael went to the Summer Olympics in Beijing, China. He planned to swim in eight events. His **goal** was to win eight gold **medals**. No one had ever won so many gold medals in one year.

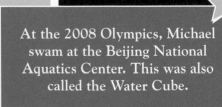

At the 2008 Olympics, Michael swam at the Beijing National Aquatics Center. This was also called the Water Cube.

In 1972, Mark Spitz won seven Olympic gold medals. Michael wanted to win eight and make a new record!

23

Some people believe Michael's ADHD helped him focus on his goal. People with ADHD can be especially focused on one certain interest or goal.

At the Olympics, Michael swam 17 races in nine days. Swimming in so many different races is very **challenging**. People were excited to watch Michael race.

Many races were close. But, Michael accomplished his **goal** and won eight gold **medals**! He also set seven world records!

Michael's mother is one of his biggest fans. She is proud of her son's accomplishments.

Star Swimmer

Michael's swimming skill has made him famous. He has appeared on magazine covers, such as *Sports Illustrated*. He has also been on television shows, such as *Saturday Night Live*.

Some people say Michael is the greatest swimmer ever. He has broken many world records for speed. And, he has won 48 medals. Forty of these are gold medals. And 14 are Olympic gold!

Michael continues training with Bob
at the North Baltimore Aquatic Club.

Buzz

In 2007, Michael bought a home in Fells Point, Maryland. This is near Baltimore. There, Michael is preparing for the 2012 Olympics. He swims every day to keep his body strong. Fans are excited to see what's next for Michael Phelps!

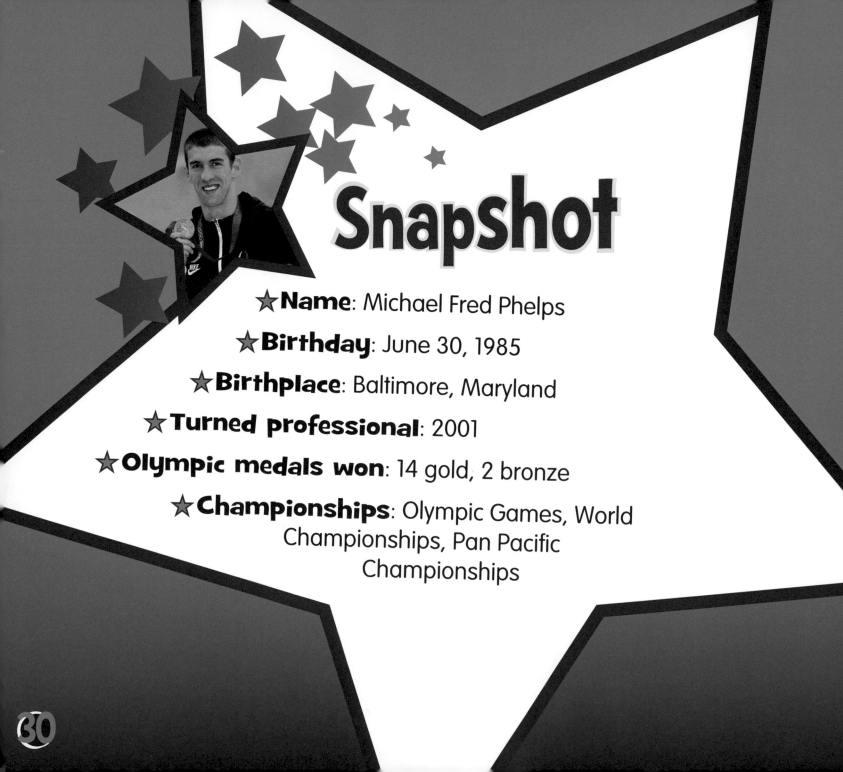

Snapshot

★**Name**: Michael Fred Phelps

★**Birthday**: June 30, 1985

★**Birthplace**: Baltimore, Maryland

★**Turned professional**: 2001

★**Olympic medals won**: 14 gold, 2 bronze

★**Championships**: Olympic Games, World Championships, Pan Pacific Championships

Important Words

challenging testing one's strength or abilities.

championship a game, a match, or a race held to find a first-place winner.

coach someone who teaches or trains a person or a group on a certain subject or skill.

competition a contest between two or more persons or groups.

goal something that a person works to accomplish.

medal an award for success.

professional (pruh-FEHSH-nuhl) working for money rather than for pleasure.

Web Sites

To learn more about Michael Phelps, visit ABDO Publishing Company online. Web sites about Michael Phelps are featured on our Book Links page. These links are routinely monitored and updated to provide the most current information available.

www.abdopublishing.com

Index